Contents

Introduction 1
   Types of Deposit-Related Credit 1
      Check Credit 1
      Overdraft Protection 2
      Deposit Advance Products 3
      Other Products and Services 4
   Risks Associated With Deposit-Related Credit 4
      Strategic Risk 4
      Credit Risk 5
      Operational Risk 5
      Compliance Risk 6
      Reputation Risk 8
      Liquidity Risk 8
   Risk Management 8
      Management and Supervision 9
      Underwriting and Account Eligibility Criteria 10
      Monitoring and Reporting 11
      Portfolio Quality 12
      Third-Party Management 13

Examination Procedures 15
   Scope 15
   Functional Area Procedures 18
   Conclusions 32
   Internal Control Questionnaire for Check Credit 34
   Verification Procedures 38

Appendixes 39
   Appendix A: Sample Request Letter 39
   Appendix B: Checklist for Deposit Advance Products 42
   Appendix C: Abbreviations 45

References 46

Introduction

The Office of the Comptroller of the Currency's (OCC) *Comptroller's Handbook* booklet, "Deposit-Related Credit," is prepared for use by OCC examiners in connection with their examination and supervision of national banks and federal savings associations (collectively, banks). Each bank is different and may present specific issues. Accordingly, examiners should apply the information in this booklet consistent with each bank's individual circumstances.[1] When it is necessary to distinguish between them, national banks and federal savings associations are referred to separately.

Banks may offer customers a variety of small-dollar, unsecured credit products and services that are related to their deposit accounts. These deposit-related credit (DRC) products and services generally take one of three forms: check credit (CC), overdraft protection (ODP), and deposit advance products (DAP). Examiners should be aware that laws, regulations, and supervisory guidance referenced in this booklet may not apply to all DRC products and services.

Types of Deposit-Related Credit

Check Credit

CC is defined, for purposes of this booklet, as the granting of unsecured revolving lines of credit to customers. Banks provide CC products and services by three basic methods:

- **Overdraft line of credit:** This is the most common method. The bank automatically transfers funds from an existing line of credit to the customer's demand deposit account when a check or payment is presented that would cause the customer's account to be overdrawn. Transfers normally are made in stated increments, up to a bank-approved maximum line of credit, and the customer is notified that the funds have been transferred.
- **Cash reserve:** The customer must request that the bank transfer funds from an existing line of credit to the customer's demand deposit account. To avoid overdrawing the account, the customer must request the funds transfer before negotiating a check or payment against the demand deposit account.
- **Special draft:** This involves the customer negotiating a special check drawn directly against an existing line of credit, such as a credit card. Demand deposit accounts are not affected because no funds enter or leave a demand deposit account.

In all three CC methods, the bank periodically provides the customer with statements of account activity. The customer's required minimum payments are computed as a fraction of

---

[1] Pursuant to Title X of the Dodd–Frank Wall Street Reform and Consumer Protection Act of 2010 (Dodd–Frank), the Consumer Financial Protection Bureau (CFPB) is responsible for examining banks with assets over $10 billion for compliance with federal consumer financial laws (as that term is defined in Title X).

the account balance on the cycle date and are usually made by automatic charges to the demand account. Refer to the "Risk Management" section of this booklet for details.

Banks should have policies and procedures for CC products and services that include eligibility or underwriting criteria to obtain the product or service.

Overdraft Protection

Many banks offer ODP to pay customers' checks and allow other overdrafts when there are insufficient funds in the account. Common names for ODP are automated overdraft protection, bounced check protection, and courtesy overdraft protection. These are typically automated services provided to transaction account customers as alternatives to a traditional overdraft line of credit.

In most cases, customers who meet a bank's eligibility criteria may be enrolled in ODP. Banks generally do not underwrite ODP on an individual account basis when enrolling the customer. Most banks do review individual customer accounts periodically to determine whether the customer continues to qualify for the service and whether the amount of ODP coverage provided continues to be appropriate. Automation is typically used to apply specific bank criteria for determining whether to honor overdrafts and to set limits on the amount of ODP coverage provided. Some banks may supplement their ODP automated systems, however, by allowing individual officers or employees to approve overdrafts on a case-by-case basis. Many banks inform customers that payment of an overdraft is discretionary on the banks' part, and deposit account agreements typically disclose that the banks have no legal obligation to pay any overdrafts.

Some banks may extend the ODP to non-check transactions including account withdrawals made at automated teller machines (ATM), purchases using a debit card, pre-authorized automatic debits from a customer's account, automated clearing house (ACH) transactions, telephone-initiated funds transfers, or online banking transactions. Banks must provide consumers with the right to opt in, or affirmatively consent, to the bank's ODP for ATM and one-time debit card transactions (12 CFR 1005.17(b)). Notice of the opt-in right must be provided, and the consumer's affirmative consent obtained, before fees or charges may be assessed on the consumer's account for paying such overdrafts.

Fees vary by bank for ODP services and are subject to change. Banks typically charge a flat fee each time an overdraft item is paid, although some banks have a tiered fee structure and charge higher fees as the number of overdrafts increases. Banks commonly charge the same amount for paying a check or an ACH overdraft as they would if they returned the item unpaid.

National banks are authorized to provide overdraft credit relating to commercial demand deposit accounts under 12 USC 24(Seventh). A federal savings association also may extend overdraft credit. All banks are subject to the lending limitations of 12 CFR 32. Overdraft credit extended by a federal savings association relating to commercial demand deposit accounts, however, is subject to the statutory limit on commercial loans, as set forth in the

Home Owners' Loan Act (12 USC 1464(c)(2)(A)) and regulations (12 CFR 160.30, endnote 19). Management and the boards of federal savings associations should be aware of any implications and limits regarding small business loans in the calculation of the limit on commercial loans.

The interagency Joint Guidance on Overdraft Protection Programs[2] and OCC Bulletin 2010-15, "Overdraft Protection: Opt-In Requirements and Related Marketing Issues," apply to bank ODP. Laws, regulations, and supervisory guidance pertaining to ODP are subject to change, and bank management, directors, and examiners are encouraged to stay informed and up to date. Existing regulations cover a variety of topics related to overdrafts, such as disclosures concerning fees, account-opening disclosures, and advertising rules.

Deposit Advance Products

A DAP is a type of small-dollar, short-term credit product offered to customers maintaining a deposit account, reloadable prepaid card, or similar deposit-related vehicle at a bank. The bank provides a credit feature that allows the customer to take out a loan in advance of the customer's next direct deposit. The advance is based on a history of the customer's recurring deposits. Typically, the advance is offered as an open-end line of credit; OCC guidance on DAPs, however, applies to all such extensions of credit, whether the product is structured as open- or closed-end credit.[3] Specific details of DAPs vary among banks and may vary over time. Historically, DAPs incorporate some or all of the following general characteristics, a number of which have been addressed in OCC Bulletin 2013-40, "Deposit Advance Products: Final Supervisory Guidance.

- **Cost:** The cost is based on a fee structure, rather than an interest rate. Advances are made in fixed dollar increments and a flat fee is assessed for each advance. For example, a DAP may be structured so that a customer may obtain advances in increments of $20 with a fee of $10 per every $100 advanced.
- **Eligibility and loan limits:** A customer is eligible for a DAP if the deposit account has been open for a certain period and the customer receives recurring deposits. Banks generally require that a minimum sum be directly deposited each month for a certain period for the customer to be eligible for a DAP. The minimum deposit and time period may vary by bank. The maximum dollar amount of the DAP generally is limited to a percentage or amount of the recurring deposit.
- **Ability to repay:** Some DAPs have been predicated solely on the amount and frequency of a customer's deposits, rather than the customer's ability to repay.
- **Repayment:** Repayment is required through a preauthorized electronic payment of the advance and the fee with each deposit; however, some banks have implemented alternative repayment methods, such as the customer mailing the payment or coming into the bank to make the payment. The bank is paid before any other transactions are paid. If

---

[2] OCC Bulletin 2005-9, "Overdraft Protection Programs: Interagency Guidance," 70 Fed. Reg. 9127 (2005).

[3] OCC Bulletin 2013-40, "Deposit Advance Products: Final Supervisory Guidance."

the first deposit is insufficient to repay the advance and the fee, the repayment is obtained from subsequent deposits.

- **Marketing and access:** Banks market DAPs as intended to assist customers with financial emergencies or to meet short-term needs. These advances are typically not included with the banks' lists of available credit products but instead are listed as a deposit account feature.

OCC Bulletin 2013-40 sets forth the OCC's risk management expectations for DAPs.

Other Products and Services

Some banks implement unsecured credit products and services in the form of installment loans in place of DAPs. See the *Comptroller's Handbook* booklet "Installment Loans" for additional information on unsecured lending.

Risks Associated With Deposit-Related Credit

From a supervisory perspective, risk is the potential that events, expected or unexpected, will have an adverse effect on a bank's earnings, capital, or franchise or enterprise value. The OCC has defined eight categories of risk for bank supervision purposes: credit, interest rate, liquidity, price, operational, compliance, strategic, and reputation. These categories are not mutually exclusive. Any product or service may expose a bank to multiple risks. Risks also may be interdependent and may be positively or negatively correlated. Examiners should be aware of this interdependence and assess the effect of risks in a consistent and inclusive manner. Refer to the "Bank Supervision Process" booklet of the *Comptroller's Handbook* for an expanded discussion of banking risks and their definitions.

DRC can be offered in a safe and sound manner if bank management properly understands and controls its primary risks: strategic, credit, operational, and compliance. Failure to control the primary risks of DRC products and services may contribute to other risks, such as reputation and liquidity. Poorly structured DRC products and services can pose harm to customers. Accordingly, DRC products and services should be carefully designed and managed.

Strategic Risk

A bank assumes strategic risk when taking on new product lines without having the expertise and systems to properly manage and control risks associated with the line of business. In a sound DRC program, management ensures that staff has the knowledge and experience to recognize, assess, mitigate, and monitor the bank's DRC risks. Failure to provide effective oversight of DRC activities can increase the bank's strategic risk profile while also negatively affecting interrelated risks, such as credit and reputation risks. Factors that could raise a bank's level of strategic risk include:

- Failure to provide adequate resources for DRC products and services and related control functions.
- Weaknesses in the administration of acquisitions, mergers, and alliances.

Credit Risk

DRC is generally unsecured credit, and repayment depends primarily on a customer's capacity to repay. With regard to DAP and ODP, repayment is expected from the next deposit made to the customer's account. By contrast, CC may only require the customer to make minimum monthly payments that are computed as a fraction of the outstanding balances. Customers may become overextended and unable to repay.

DRC products and services, particularly ODP and DAP, may exhibit higher-risk characteristics. Some customers who obtain certain ODP or DAP products or services may have cash flow difficulties or blemished or insufficient credit histories that limit other borrowing options. In addition, some DRC products and services (in particular, ODP) are not underwritten for the individual customer and may rely on other eligibility criteria rather than ability to repay. Extensions of credit that are subject to less stringent underwriting requirements and loans that exhibit subprime credit characteristics reflect higher risk. The structure of DRC products and services and the presence of higher-risk characteristics may increase the credit risk of individual DRC extensions of credit and of the overall DRC portfolio.

Numerous and repeated extensions of credit to the same customer may be substantially similar to continuous advances and can subject the bank to increased credit risk. Customers may repeatedly use DRC products and services if they are unable to fully repay the balance on prior extensions of credit. OCC Bulletin 2013-40 notes that this practice can be similar to the practice of "loan flipping," which the OCC, the Federal Deposit Insurance Corporation (FDIC), and the Board of Governors of the Federal Reserve System (Board) have previously noted to be an element of predatory lending.[4]

Operational Risk

On a daily basis, banks face operational risk as they process DRC for customers. Operational risk can arise for various reasons, such as a bank's failure to process a transaction properly, inadequate controls, employee error or malfeasance, a breakdown in the bank's computer system, or a natural catastrophe. Fraud also poses operational risk.

Products and services such as ODP and DAP, which are often highly automated and have a large transactional volume, require strong operational controls. To control operational risk, the bank should maintain effective internal controls and use comprehensive management information systems (MIS). Bank management should be aware that aggressive growth has

---

[4] OCC Bulletin 2001-6, "Subprime Lending: Expanded Guidance for Subprime Lending Programs." This guidance was jointly signed by the OCC, the Board, the FDIC, and the Office of Thrift Supervision (OTS).

the potential to stretch operational capacity and can cause problems in handling customer accounts.

Compliance Risk

DRC can pose significant compliance risk if a bank's systems of identifying, measuring, monitoring, and controlling risk are deficient. While compliance risk may occur at the bank level, this risk also can exist when DRC products, services, or systems associated with a third-party relationship are not properly reviewed for compliance or when the operations of the third-party relationship are not consistent with applicable law, regulations, supervisory guidance, or the bank's policies and procedures.[5]

The potential for serious or frequent violations of law, or failure to meet expectations contained in pertinent guidance, is heightened when the bank's oversight program does not include appropriate audit and control features, particularly when a third party is implementing new bank activities or expanding existing ones. Compliance risk also increases when privacy or customer records are not adequately protected, when conflicts of interest between the bank and affiliated third parties are not appropriately managed, or when the bank or its service providers have not implemented an appropriate information security program. Further, section 5 of the Federal Trade Commission Act (FTC Act), 15 USC 45, prohibits unfair or deceptive acts or practices[6] (UDAP). DRC products and services may raise UDAP concerns, depending on how they are marketed and implemented. The prohibition on UDAP applies not only to the product or service, but also to every stage of the product or service life cycle and every activity, including product development, the creation and rollout of marketing campaigns, servicing, and collections. Banks should involve their compliance management function in the due diligence and monitoring process when third-party products or services are present.

Various practices may raise compliance risk and supervisory concerns. Examples include:

- Steering customers toward DRC products and services when they may qualify for other, less costly forms of credit.
- Failure to disclose the costs and fees of DRC products and services.
- Failure to monitor accounts for excessive use of DRC products and services and the costs of those products and services.
- Failure to ensure adequate risk management, including appropriate internal audits and compliance reviews.

---

[5] On supervisory expectations for managing third-party relationships, see OCC Bulletin 2013-29, "Third-Party Relationships: Risk Management Guidance" and the "Third-Party Management" section of this booklet.

[6] For federal savings associations, see *OTS Examination Handbook* section 1354, "Unfair or Deceptive Acts or Practices, Federal Trade Commission Act, Section 5" and related "Program" and "Questionnaire." For national banks and federal savings associations, see OCC Advisory Letter 2002-3, "Guidance on Unfair or Deceptive Acts or Practices" and OCC Advisory Letter 2000-7, "Abusive Lending Practices."

- Failure to adequately disclose transaction clearing policies and failure to disclose how those policies can affect the total amount of fees associated with DRC products and services.

Other laws and regulations that may apply to one or more types of DRC include, but are not limited to, the following:[7]

- **Truth in Lending Act (TILA):** TILA and Regulation Z require creditors to provide cost disclosures for extensions of consumer credit.[8] Different rules apply to Regulation Z disclosures depending on whether the credit is an open- or closed-end credit product.
- **Electronic Fund Transfer Act (EFTA):** A DRC product or service that involves the use of electronic fund transfers must meet the applicable disclosure and other requirements of EFTA and Regulation E.[9] EFTA requires that certain disclosures be made,[10] generally prohibits creditors from mandating that credit be repaid by "preauthorized electronic fund transfers,"[11] and allows consumers to withdraw authorization for "preauthorized fund transfers."[12]
- **Truth in Savings Act (TISA):** A program that involves a consumer's deposit account must meet the disclosure requirements of TISA and Regulation DD.[13] Under TISA, deposit account disclosures must include the amount of any fee that may be imposed in connection with the account and the conditions under which the fee may be imposed.[14]
- **Equal Credit Opportunity Act (ECOA):** Under ECOA and Regulation B, creditors are prohibited from discriminating against an applicant on a prohibited basis in any aspect of a credit transaction.[15] The manner in which a creditor exercises its discretion, for example, in determining the application of eligibility requirements, loss mitigation options, and fee waivers, may raise fair lending risk.

---

[7] The list is not intended to affect whether or when such laws or regulations may apply to a particular DRC product or service.

[8] 15 USC 1601 et seq. TILA is implemented by Regulation Z, 12 CFR 1026.

[9] 15 USC 1693 et seq. EFTA is implemented by Regulation E, 12 CFR 1005.

[10] See, e.g., 12 CFR 1005.7, 1005.8, and 1005.9.

[11] See 12 CFR 1005.10(e).

[12] See 12 CFR 1005.10(c).

[13] 12 USC 4301 et seq. TISA is implemented by Regulation DD at 12 CFR 1030 for depository institutions, including national banks and federal savings associations.

[14] See 12 CFR 1030.4(b)(4).

[15] 15 USC 1691 et seq. ECOA is implemented by Regulation B, 12 CFR 1002. ECOA prohibits discrimination on the basis of race, color, religion, national origin, sex, marital status, age (provided the applicant has the capacity to contract), the fact that all or part of the applicant's income derives from a public assistance program, and the fact that the applicant has in good faith exercised any right under the Consumer Credit Protection Act.

Banks involved in DRC face litigation risk, both from private lawsuits and from regulatory enforcement actions. Litigation risk is increased if DRC is not administered properly. Before implementing DRC programs, banks should have their products and services reviewed by bank counsel to ensure compliance with all applicable laws and regulations.

Examiners are reminded that laws and regulations are subject to change. Consequently, examiners should assess whether banks monitor applicable laws and regulations for revisions and ensure that the banks' services and programs remain fully compliant with such laws and regulations.

Reputation Risk

The bank should consider the possible reputation risk involved in DRC. This risk may arise from the bank's obligations to customers and contracts with third-party providers, as well as through the outsourcing of any parts of the DRC program. Any aspect of DRC that the bank or the bank's third-party providers conduct that is not consistent with the bank's policies and standards, or laws and regulations, could subject the bank to reputation risk. Adverse publicity about the product may increase reputation risk. Also, publicity about adverse events involving third-party providers may increase the bank's reputation risk. See the "Third-Party Management" section of this booklet and OCC Bulletin 2013-29, "Third-Party Relationships: Risk Management Guidance," for additional information.

Banks may be subject to negative news coverage and public scrutiny from reports of high fees and customers taking out multiple advances to cover prior advances and everyday expenses. Engaging in practices that are perceived to be unfair or detrimental to the customer can cause a bank to lose community support and business.

Liquidity Risk

Management should keep apprised of the funding requirements created by DRC products and services. Failing to do so exposes the bank to liquidity risk.

Risk Management

Each bank should identify, measure, monitor, and control risk by implementing an effective risk management system appropriate for the size and the complexity of its operations. When examiners assess the effectiveness of a bank's risk management system, they consider the bank's policies, processes, personnel, and control systems. Refer to the "Bank Supervision Process" booklet of the *Comptroller's Handbook* for an expanded discussion of risk management.

This section focuses on the primary methods by which banks manage risk. The risk management processes and controls may vary from bank to bank and may include differences by individual products and services.

Management and Supervision

The board and management of any bank considering whether to offer DRC products and services or to maintain or expand the bank's DRC program should be fully aware of the risks involved. Management should (1) identify the business activities' risks, as well as the expertise and controls required to manage them; (2) determine how well the bank can keep pace with technology and competition; and (3) determine whether the bank will use third-party organizations in the activity and, if so, how much the bank will use them, for what purposes, and for what DRC products and services.

Banks should have risk management systems commensurate with an activity's risk and complexity. Management experience, staffing, systems, and reporting should be sufficient to enable the bank to monitor the activity knowledgeably and effectively.

Management should evaluate the risk and reward for DRC activity and ensure that the bank is not taking on an unacceptable level of risk. Banks may be subject to exposure and losses through credit transactions with customers or through fraud. Uncontrolled growth and inadequate operations by third parties may further contribute to problems for banks. Management should consider the implications the activity may pose for capital and earnings.

A bank should maintain adequate oversight and exercise appropriate control over its DRC products and services so as to minimize exposure to potential financial loss, reputation damage, and supervisory action. The bank's compliance management system should consider all statutes, regulations, guidance, and internal policies and procedures applicable to the products and services offered by the bank, including DRC.

A bank should adopt policies and procedures that set forth eligibility criteria for a customer to obtain the DRC product or service.

Capital

Higher capital requirements generally apply to loan portfolios that exhibit higher-risk characteristics and are subject to less stringent loan underwriting requirements. Loan portfolios that exhibit subprime credit characteristics are higher risk and may require higher levels of capital. Any higher risk posed through contractual arrangements with third-party providers for DRC activities should be considered when determining the adequacy of capital for the activities. The board and management should limit the bank's volume of DRC relative to the bank's capital, its risk profile, and management's ability to monitor and control DRC risks.

Banks should ensure proper risk-based regulatory capital treatment of outstanding overdrawn balances and unused commitments. Overdraft balances should be risk weighted according to the obligor. Under the interagency risk-based capital rules,[16] the capital charge on the unused portion of a commitment generally is based on an off-balance-sheet credit conversion factor and the risk weight appropriate to the obligor. In general, these rules provide that the unused portion of a commitment is subject to a 20 percent credit conversion factor if the commitment has an original maturity of one year or less or a 50 percent credit conversion factor if the commitment has an original maturity of more than one year. Also, ODP that is unconditionally cancelable by banks in accordance with applicable law qualify for a 0 percent credit conversion factor.

Marketing

Account materials and marketing should not mislead customers about the optional nature of a DRC product or service or otherwise promote routine use or undue reliance on the products and services. In addition, a customer should be permitted to opt out of a DRC product or service at any time, after which no future advances may be made or related fees imposed, and the customer should be provided clear notice of this option. (See OCC Advisory Letter 2000-7, "Abusive Lending Practices," for national banks and federal savings associations. See also *OTS Examination Handbook* section 1354, "Unfair or Deceptive Acts or Practices, Federal Trade Commission Act, Section 5" [including the accompanying program and questionnaire] for federal savings associations. See OCC Advisory Letter 2002-3, "Guidance on Unfair or Deceptive Acts or Practices" for national banks and federal savings associations.)

Underwriting and Account Eligibility Criteria

Underwriting and eligibility criteria for CC and DAP should be well documented in the bank's credit policy, consistent with eligibility and underwriting criteria for other bank extensions of credit. Banks' underwriting and eligibility criteria should prevent churning and prolonged use of products and services intended to meet short-term credit needs. Repetitive use of certain CC and DAP products and services could indicate weak underwriting, may be criticized in the Report of Examination, and may affect a bank's CAMELS[17] ratings and risk assessment.

Written underwriting policies for CC and DAP generally should include an assessment of

- the length of a customer's deposit relationship with the bank.
- the customer's history with the bank on any current or prior relationships including classified credits.
- the customer's willingness and ability to repay or financial capacity.

---

[16] OCC Bulletin 2013-23, "Regulatory Capital Rule: Final Rulemaking." Subject to various transition periods, the rule became effective for advanced approaches banks on January 1, 2014, and for all other banks on January 1, 2015. Other documents included with the release of the new rule include the interagency *New Capital Rule, Community Bank Guide* and the OCC-issued *New Capital Rule Quick Reference Guide for Community Banks*.

[17] CAMELS components are capital adequacy, asset quality, management, earnings, liquidity, and sensitivity to market risk.

- factors to be considered before increasing credit limits (i.e., prior payment performance and the impact of the increase of the credit limit on the borrower's willingness and ability to repay or financial capacity).
- the customer's continuing eligibility.

Prudent ODP risk management practices include establishing express account eligibility standards and well-defined and properly documented dollar limit decision criteria. In addition, there should be established procedures for the suspension of overdraft services when the account holder no longer meets the eligibility criteria (such as when the account holder has declared bankruptcy or defaulted on other credit at the bank).

Monitoring and Reporting

Management Information Systems

Bank management should receive regular reports on the volume, trend, profitability, delinquency, and credit performance of the DRC program. These MIS reports should segment accounts by level of utilization to identify excessive product usage. Management should receive reports that describe the status and outcome of internal reviews and evaluations of accounts identified as demonstrating excessive usage.

Ongoing Monitoring and Account Management

DRC accounts should be monitored to ensure that changing customer circumstances have not adversely affected credit risk and to identify excessive usage. For ODP, banks should monitor for excessive usage, which may indicate a need for alternative credit arrangements or other services, and inform customers of available options. With respect to DAP, banks should monitor for repeated customer usage, which may indicate a need for alternative credit arrangements or other services, and inform customers of these available options when appropriate.

Banks that have extended their CC programs to small businesses have found that the practice may involve a higher than normal risk unless placed under very stringent controls. Because such advances are basically unsecured lines of credit, the examiner's review should be based on the same factors and criteria used in the review of unsecured commercial loans. See the *Comptroller's Handbook* booklet, "Commercial Loans," for additional information regarding unsecured lending.

Regulatory and Financial Reporting

With respect to the reporting of income and loss recognition, banks must follow the instructions for the Consolidated Reports of Condition and Income (call report) and generally accepted accounting principles (GAAP). Banks should adopt rigorous loss estimation processes to ensure that fee income associated with DRC is accurately measured. Such methods may include providing loss allowances for uncollectible fees or only recognizing that portion of earned fees estimated to be collectible. The procedures for estimating an adequate allowance should be documented in accordance with OCC Bulletin 2001-37, "Policy Statement on Allowance for Loan and Lease Losses Methodologies and Documentation for Banks and Savings Institutions: ALLL Methodologies and Documentation," and OCC Bulletin 2005-9, "Overdraft Protection Programs: Interagency Guidance."

If a bank advises customers of the available amount of ODP, for example, when accounts are opened, or the amount is noted on customers' account statements or ATM receipts, the bank must report the available amount of ODP coverage with legally binding commitments for call report purposes. These available amounts, therefore, must be reported as "unused commitments" in regulatory reports.

Portfolio Quality

Delinquencies

Delinquencies in CC and DAP accounts often occur when an account is at or near the maximum credit line. Accordingly, management should review frequent, comprehensive reports that reflect pertinent information about the CC or DAP product or service, including schedules of

- delinquent accounts (aged).
- accounts for which payments are made by drawing on reserves.
- accounts with steady usage.

Classification and Charge-Off

An overdraft balance generally should be charged off when considered uncollectible, but no later than 60 days from the date that balance first became overdrawn. In some cases, a bank may allow a customer to cover an overdraft through an extended repayment plan if the customer is unable to bring the account to a positive balance within the required time frame. The existence of a repayment plan, however, does not change the bank's obligation to charge off the overdraft 60 days from the date of the overdraft (or a shorter period, if warranted). Any payments received after the account is charged off (up to the amount charged off against allowance) should be reported as a recovery.

Some overdrafts may be rewritten as loan obligations in accordance with the bank's loan policy and supported by a documented assessment of the customer's ability to repay. In those instances, the charge-off time frames described in the Federal Financial Institutions Examination Council (FFIEC) Uniform Retail Credit Classification and Account Management Policy (Retail Classification Policy) apply.

Deposit advances that are not repaid in accordance with the account terms should be charged off. The OCC's policy with respect to charge-off of CC advances is the same as for charge-off of credit card advances.[18]

The FFIEC Retail Classification Policy establishes guidelines for classifying consumer credit based on delinquency, but the policy also allows discretion to classify individual retail loans that exhibit signs of credit weakness, regardless of delinquency status. An examiner also may classify retail portfolios, or segments thereof, for which underwriting standards are weak and present unreasonable credit risk. See OCC Bulletin 2000-20, "Uniform Retail Credit Classification and Account Management Policy: Policy Implementation" for additional information.

Third-Party Management

Third-party relationships include any entity the bank contracts with to provide DRC products and services. Banks frequently outsource functions to third-party relationships to control costs. Banks can benefit from the technological expertise and capabilities of third parties without having to develop the systems and infrastructure themselves. Third-party relationships provide a wide array of services; examiners should understand that each bank's list of third parties used and services outsourced is unique.

A bank's use of a third party, including technology service providers, to provide products and services does not diminish the responsibility of the bank's board of directors and management to ensure that the activities are conducted in a safe and sound manner and in compliance with applicable laws and regulations, just as if the bank were to perform the activities in-house.

The quality of the services provided by third-party relationships can vary widely. Banks should exercise due diligence and maintain ongoing monitoring of the third party's activities and performance.

Banks should have risk management processes that are commensurate with the level of risk and complexity of its third-party relationships and the bank's organizational structures. More comprehensive and rigorous oversight and management are appropriate for third-party relationships that involve critical activities, for example, significant bank functions (such as payments, clearing, settlements, or custody) and significant shared services (such as information technology), or other activities that

- could cause a bank to face significant risk if the third party fails to meet expectations.
- could have significant negative impact on customers.
- require significant investment in resources to implement the third-party relationship and manage the risk.

---

[18] OCC Bulletin 2000-20, "Uniform Retail Credit Classification and Account Management Policy: Policy Implementation."

- could have a major impact on bank operations if the bank has to find an alternate third party to conduct the outsourced activity or if the outsourced activity has to be brought in-house.

Banks should conduct appropriate due diligence before selecting a third-party provider. Regardless of the type of third-party relationship, selecting a competent and qualified third-party provider is essential to managing third-party risk. The due diligence process provides the bank with an opportunity to review qualitative and quantitative aspects, both financial and operational, of a third party and to assess whether the third party can help the bank achieve its strategic goals.

Bank management should periodically arrange for on-site inspections and audits of third-party organizations. Written audit reports should be generated, and the third party's management should be required to respond in writing to issues identified during inspections and audits. If the third party is required to have specialized audits or an attestation engagement (e.g., an attestation engagement according to the Statement on Standards for Attestation Engagement No. 16, "Reporting on Controls at a Service Organization" [SSAE 16]) or elects to have such audits or attestation, bank management should obtain and review the audits or attestation.

Examiners and bank management should refer to OCC Bulletin 2013-29, "Third-Party Relationships: Risk Management Guidance," and booklets including the "Supervision of Technology Service Providers" and "Outsourcing Technology Services" of the *FFIEC Information Technology (IT) Examination Handbook* for additional guidance. The agencies' "Administrative Guidelines—Implementation of Interagency Programs for the Supervision of Technology Service Providers" is another reference document that can be consulted.

Banks also should ensure that third-party processors and network providers have contingency plans for continuing operations. Examiners conducting reviews of this area should include IT examiners to the extent needed to review the bank's in-house data-processing systems and the adequacy of the business continuity and contingency plan.

Examination Procedures

This booklet contains expanded procedures for examining specialized activities or specific products or services that warrant extra attention beyond the core assessment contained in the "Community Bank Supervision," "Large Bank Supervision," and "Federal Branches and Agencies Supervision" booklets of the *Comptroller's Handbook*. Examiners determine which expanded procedures to use, if any, during examination planning or after drawing preliminary conclusions during the core assessment.

Scope

These procedures are designed to help examiners tailor the examination to each bank and determine the scope of the DRC examination. This determination should consider work performed by internal and external auditors and other independent risk control functions and by other examiners on related areas. Examiners need to perform only the objectives and steps that are relevant to the scope of the examination as determined by the following objective. Examinations seldom require every objective or step of the procedures.

Objective: To determine the scope of the DRC examination and identify the objectives and activities necessary to the supervisory strategy for the bank.

1. Review the following documents to identify any issues that require follow-up. Consider

    *   previous DRC and compliance examinations findings and management's response to those findings; these findings may relate to CC, ODP, DAP, or other applicable products and services.
    *   work performed by internal and external auditors, internal and external loan review, and credit examiners, including reports issued and management's response to significant deficiencies.
    *   supervisory strategy and the scope memorandum issued by the bank's examiner-in-charge (EIC).
    *   work papers from the previous examination.

2. Obtain and review management information related to the supervision of DRC activities, focusing on any significant changes or trends since the last examination. Consider

    *   the bank's current plans, both formal and informal, that relate to DRC products and services.
    *   management's analysis of capital adequacy or capital allocated for DRC risks.
    *   an organizational chart including each functional area.
    *   copies of formal job descriptions for all personnel involved with the DRC products and services.
    *   copies of the two most recent monthly management reports provided to the board of directors for DRC products and services.

- copies of all internal and external audit reports issued since the last examination, with any response from management.
- copies of all loan review and ODP reports for the DRC products and services.
- new customer accounts reports for the applicable products for the previous three months.
- a list of board and executive or senior management committees that supervise DRC products and services, including a list of members and copies of minutes documenting those meetings since the last examination.
- copies of marketing plans for the overall DRC products and services and, if applicable, for each DRC product and service.
- copies of applicable policies and procedures for DRC products and services.
- profitability reports for the specific DRC products and services for the most recent year-end and year to date.
- a list of all insiders who have DRC or receive DRC products and services.
- any management reports addressing credit risk posed by specific DRC products and services, as well as reports addressing credit risk associated with customers that have those products and services.
- daily fraud-monitoring reports.
- fraud loss and credit loss history (including information concerning ODP losses).
- list of third-party organizations that provide DRC-related services to the bank, including name and address of each third-party organization, and a description of services provided by them related to the applicable product.
- customer complaints filed with the bank, and other entities, in connection with applicable DRC products and services.

3. Identify, during early discussions with management,

- any significant changes in policies, practices, personnel, staffing, and controls since the last DRC examination.
- what DRC program(s) are offered and whether the programs were developed and administered internally or externally.
- any changes in the bank's DRC-related activities (e.g., products, services, growth, geographies, target market, marketing plan and activities, and third-party providers and vendors associated with the bank's DRC products and services).
- how management supervises product and service operations.
- any internal or external factors that could affect operations.

4. Using the findings derived from performing the preceding procedures and from information obtained during discussions with the bank's EIC and other appropriate supervisors, set the examination's scope and objectives. From the following examination procedures, internal control questions, and verification procedures, select the ones necessary to meet those objectives.

5. As examination procedures are performed, test for compliance with the bank's established policies, procedures, internal controls, and applicable laws and regulations, and consistency with OCC issuances. Identify any area with inadequate supervision, weak internal controls, undue risk, or increasing risk profile.

Functional Area Procedures

Overall objective: To assess the quantity and direction of risks in a bank's DRC activity; understand management's risk appetite; gain an understanding of products and services offered or planned; assess policies, procedures, and practices used in DRC; and assess compliance with applicable laws and regulations and consistency with OCC guidance.

This objective is achieved through completion of examination activities in some or all of the following functional areas.

Separate from these Functional Area Procedures, compliance-specific procedures may be found in the Consumer Compliance series of booklets of the *Comptroller's Handbook*. Compliance-specific booklets are generally arranged according to specific regulations. A number of compliance regulations may be applicable to DRC products and services. See the Compliance Risk section in the Introduction of this booklet for additional information.

Management and Supervision

Objective: To assess the adequacy of the strategic plan, business plan, and overall planning process, including management's methodology for setting DRC growth and profitability targets, and the processes to ensure appropriate expertise and sufficient staffing within the DRC line of business.

1. Review the bank's strategic and business plans and determine whether management's plans for DRC products and services are clear and represent the current direction of the bank, as well as any changes since the last examination that may not be consistent with the bank's current strategic plan.

2. If issues identified in prior examinations, audits, or credit reviews remain uncorrected, determine whether the board or its audit committee has adopted a corrective action plan and, if so, the status of implementing corrective actions.

3. Obtain, through discussion with the manager of the DRC activities, information about the overall portfolio, MIS, and policies. Review significant changes since the last examination to understand how the changes have affected the portfolio's risk profile.

4. Evaluate any new programs the bank is pursuing and what effect the programs may have on the DRC operation.

5. Review all aspects of the DRC programs offered by the bank, including marketing practices, advertising, and customer disclosures, to ensure that they are consistent with applicable laws, rules, regulations, and with OCC guidance.

6. Assess performance management and compensation programs. Consider whether these programs measure and reward performance that aligns with the bank's strategic objectives and risk appetite.

- If the bank offers incentive compensation programs, determine whether they are consistent with applicable rules and guidance. OCC Bulletin 2010-24, "Interagency Guidance on Sound Incentive Compensation Policies," provides that incentive compensation arrangements should comply with the following three key principles:
  - Provide employees with incentives that appropriately balance risk and reward.
  - Be compatible with effective controls and risk management.
  - Be supported by strong corporate governance, including active and effective oversight by the bank's board of directors.

7. Assess management's responsiveness to regulatory, accounting, industry, and technological changes.

8. Review the organizational chart for the department or line of business to determine what other responsibilities, if any, the DRC manager has within the bank. Determine whether the organizational structure is appropriate.

9. Determine what committees, if any, are involved in reviewing DRC products and services. Review the committee's minutes for pertinent information about discussion of risks, changes to current products and services, and any potential new products and services being considered. Determine whether the committee structures, if any, are appropriate.

10. Determine whether current staffing levels meet the bank's short- and long-term requirements. Determine whether

    - staffing levels are adequate for the number of accounts, volume of activity on the accounts, account monitoring needs, and, if applicable, the need to oversee third parties and use of outsourcing arrangements for the DRC products and services.
    - staffing levels are sufficient to investigate daily fraud exception reports in a timely manner.
    - turnover of staff for the area appears high and, if so, why.

11. Determine whether there is a separate bank policy for DRC products and services or if it is incorporated within another bank policy. If there is a separate policy, determine when it was approved by the board of directors and when it was last updated.

12. Evaluate the overall adequacy of written policies for DRC products and services by considering whether the policy

    - establishes clear lines of authority and responsibility.
    - identifies the risks the bank is willing to accept and limits the amount of those risks in relation to capital or earnings, as appropriate.
    - provides for adequate and knowledgeable staff.
    - requires written contracts between all third parties associated with DRC products and services.

- establishes underwriting or eligibility criteria, as appropriate, applied to qualify customer accounts for DRC products and services, and for the acceptance of new customer accounts into DRC products and services.
- requires the development of procedures to monitor the activity of customer accounts.
- establishes risk-based guidelines for the periodic review of customer accounts.
- requires adequate MIS to keep management and the board informed of the DRC program's condition.
- requires a comprehensive procedure manual to guide officers and employees in administering the DRC program.
- establishes guidelines for handling exceptions to policy (including appropriate approval and monitoring requirements and criteria for suspending availability), and sets limits on acceptable exception volumes.
- addresses criteria for paying DRC items, such as overdrafts or debit items.
- establishes appropriate limits for DRC items in conjunction with different types of deposit accounts. For example, limits with overdrafts might include dollar limits for individual items and cumulative items, and item limits, such as the number of overdraft items that are allowed during a statement cycle or other specific time frame or during the life of the account.
- establishes guidelines for a cooling off period for DAP products.
- establishes criteria for canceling participation and privileges in DRC products and services, as well as criteria for the charge-off of an ODP balance or outstanding balances on other DRC products and services.
- identifies circumstances under which features of a DRC program or product are reactivated for suspended or canceled customer accounts, if applicable.
- establishes criteria for establishing a payment plan for a customer using certain DRC products and services, if the bank offers a payment plan option.

13. Determine whether DRC policies are approved and annually reviewed by the board of directors or a committee thereof. Determine whether the board, or a committee thereof, evaluates policies for changing market and business conditions at least annually and whether the policies are in line with the overall strategic plan for this activity.

14. Determine whether the bank policy addresses charge-off requirements and accounting treatment for DRC products and services and assess the policy's appropriateness. Also, determine whether the bank uses the same charge-off time frames for all DRC products and services or whether it varies by product.

15. Determine whether the bank policy addresses the approval process for new DRC accounts, including any applicable underwriting or account eligibility criteria for new accounts. Determine whether the policy addresses the following items:

- Documentation requirements for customer files.
- Applicable underwriting for DAP or CC, or ODP account eligibility criteria guidelines, for customer accounts.
- Guidelines for suspending DRC accounts.

- Termination or closing procedures for DRC accounts.
- Types of derogatory information acceptable on credit reports, if applicable.
- Handling of exceptions for DRC account approvals.

16. Determine whether the board has adopted a policy applicable to small businesses for underwriting new DRC accounts, or determining eligibility criteria for ODP. If so, determine whether the policy states that

- the customer must provide the bank with financial information, the type of information, and the frequency of obtaining the information (if this occurs on a periodic basis after the account is opened).
- an experienced commercial credit officer must review the periodic financial statements of the business.
- the bank must review the depth and experience of the management of the business.
- the bank must perform required background checks and that the checks should determine whether any business or the business's principals have criminal records.

Underwriting and Account Eligibility Criteria

Objective: To determine whether underwriting standards (for CC and DAP) and account eligibility criteria (for ODP) are consistent with business and strategic plans, as well as risk appetite objectives, and whether appropriate controls and systems are in place. To assess the quality of new DRC accounts, identify any changes from past underwriting standards or account eligibility criteria, determine the adequacy of and adherence to DRC policies and procedures, and gain a thorough understanding of the processes employed in DRC underwriting and account eligibility criteria.

1. Evaluate the bank's policy and process for approving new DRC accounts, including underwriting or account eligibility criteria for new accounts. Determine whether the policy addresses the following items:

- Types of customer accounts for which the bank does not want to offer DRC products and services.
- Documentation requirements for DRC files.
- Underwriting or eligibility criteria guidelines for DRC products and services, including approval of line or limit increases for DRC products and services.
- Criteria to ensure that extensions of credit and fees can be timely repaid.
- Termination or closing account procedures for DRC accounts and services.
- What types of derogatory information from credit reports may be acceptable, if applicable.
- Handling of exceptions to the DRC account and service approval policy.

2. Determine what information sources the bank relies upon to evaluate a customer's creditworthiness for CC or DAP, or account eligibility for ODP, and the extent to which

the bank relies upon information solely or in conjunction with other forms of information. Evaluate whether the bank relies on

- information provided by the customer through an application.
- information provided through a credit bureau report and whether the bank evaluates the information from the report.
- a credit score. Banks may use credit scores or credit bureau information to project the probability of future payment performance based on past experience, but are not required to do so.
- a proprietary scoring model and, if so, determine what factors and information are considered in the model.
- an evaluation of a customer's account behavior based on inflows and outflows through deposit accounts.

3. Determine whether the bank's underwriting policies and practices for a CC or DAP product or service, and its eligibility criteria for an ODP service, are commensurate with the specific risks associated with the product type and the terms and conditions under which the product will be extended. Underwriting and eligibility policies and practices among banks may vary, but should be appropriate based on the type of credit product.

- Evaluate whether the bank is conducting an appropriate degree of analysis before a customer's request for credit is approved to determine whether the customer will be able to manage and repay the credit obligations in accordance with the terms associated with the product.
- Determine whether the bank's DAP underwriting requirements evaluate whether the customer will have sufficient remaining funds after making scheduled payments to cover necessary and recurring living expenses.
- Evaluate the terms of the DRC product to determine whether product features increase the probability that a customer will be able to successfully manage repayment of the obligation.

4. Evaluate the bank's procedures for ensuring compliance with the DRC approval policy.

5. Determine how the bank documents and monitors exceptions to the DRC approval policy. Evaluate the practices for waiving documentation requirements.

6. Select a representative sample of recently approved DRC files (for example, within the last 90 days). Review the sample of files for compliance with the bank's underwriting policies or practices, or account eligibility criteria, and consistency with OCC guidance. See appendix B for a "Checklist for Deposit Advance Products" to aid in the sample review. Summarize the results of the DRC file review. Determine whether the level of exceptions is reasonable in view of board-approved policies.

7. Obtain the following reports, which may be used in step 8 and for sampling and testing purposes:

- Most recent report of overlimit and overline accounts (list of any DRC accounts for which the bank customer has exceeded the established limit and line granted by the bank for the account).
- Most recent exception reports.
- Most recent stagnant maximum usage report.
- Most recent inactive suspects report (list of accounts on which payments are made by drawing on reserves).
- Most recent report of customers who have opted in/opted out of ODP products and services.
- Month-end account balance and total delinquency.
- Trial balance of all accounts related to the DRC area. Using the trial balance (if needed for verification purposes),
  - agree or reconcile balances to departmental controls and general ledger. If the totals do not agree or reconcile, it may be necessary to obtain support records for daily transactions that may have posted later and account for a difference in the totals.
  - review reconciling items for reasonableness.

8. Using appropriate sampling techniques, select customers with DRC products and services for review. Review the selected accounts, preparing line sheets or worksheets where appropriate, and

- if the credit was granted since the preceding examination, ascertain that the
  - application form is on file and properly completed.
  - customer's signature is on file.
  - credit check or review of eligibility criteria has been performed, if required for the particular product.
  - established credit limit is properly authorized and in compliance with policies.
- test the accuracy of the reports obtained at step 7 by
  - tracing any overlimit credit for proper inclusion in the overline report. For those included, review the files to determine whether
    - the line or limit was originally established in compliance with bank policy.
    - the overline or overlimit status was the result of deficiencies in policy or procedures.
    - action has been taken to prohibit additional advances until the account is within the established credit line.
    - based upon available information, customer has the ability to repay or meets account eligibility criteria (which may vary by product).
  - tracing credits with exceptions for proper inclusion in appropriate exception reports. For those included, determine whether appropriate action is being taken to resolve the situation and whether collectability is questionable.
  - tracing any long-standing fully advanced credits for proper inclusion in the stagnant maximum usage report. For those included, determine whether appropriate action is being taken to resolve the situation and whether collectability is questionable.

- tracing any delinquent credit for proper inclusion in the appropriate past-due report.
- review accounts selected to determine adequacy of and compliance with bank policy and procedures for
  - granting of extensions.
  - identification of outstanding balances on any DRC accounts carried forward or rolled over to other credits, when the prior credit amount was not paid in a timely fashion.
  - placing accounts on reduced payments schedule.
  - placing accounts on nonaccrual status.
  - cooling off periods, if applicable.
  - identification of excessive, repeated usage of products and services.

9. In evaluating the bank's ongoing review of DRC accounts, determine

- the type or size of DRC accounts included for review.
- what area of the bank conducts the review and the frequency of the review.
- the scope of the review and the bank's documentation process for the review.
- if the review covers DRC accounts for business customers, whether the review is coordinated with the commercial loan department.

Portfolio Quality

Objective: To evaluate portfolio quality and the effectiveness of charge-off processes for DRC. To ensure the bank complies with laws, rules, and regulations, and consistency with supervisory guidance.

1. Obtain the reports listed below for the DRC products and services. These reports may be used to identify credits that potentially should be charged off, to evaluate portfolio quality, or in conjunction with a review for compliance with laws and regulations and consistency with supervisory guidance and bank policy. The use of some of these reports may be more fully addressed in procedures elsewhere under this section.

- Past-due credits.
- Overdraft report.
- Use of DRC products and services by major shareholders, employees, executive officers, directors, or their related interests.
- Extensions of credit to officers and directors of other banks.
- Miscellaneous loan debit and credit suspense accounts.
- DRCs considered problem credits by management.
- Specific guidelines in the bank's lending policy.
- Each officer's current lending authority.
- Current interest rate structure.
- Any useful information obtained from the minutes of the loan and discount committee or any similar committee for DRC products and services.

- Reports furnished to the loan, retail banking, or other appropriate committee.
- Reports furnished to the board of directors.

2. Review the overdraft report and determine whether charge-offs are taken in accordance with bank policy and consistent with supervisory guidance. Verify that management has established reasonable loss recognition guidelines. Overdrafts should generally be charged off within 60 days after the date the account first went into overdraft status. Stale items that appear on the overdraft report should be charged off.

3. If the bank does not have a periodic charge-off policy, the bank should develop and implement one. Prepare a list of stale and past-due DRC items for discussion with management and direct charge-off as appropriate. The list should include the customer name, account number, amount outstanding, loan or account identification number, and any other pertinent information.

4. Review reports for any past-due credits for the DRC area since the previous examination and investigate any significant variations.

5. If the bank uses repayment plans to allow customers longer terms to pay off overdrafts, determine whether the accounts are carried on the books beyond 60 days from the date of the advance. Those accounts should be charged off and the subsequent plan payments treated as an allowance recovery.

6. Review charge-offs and recoveries over the last year. If the bank does not have appropriate MIS to track trends, calculate the ratio on a quarterly or semiannual basis as appropriate. Evaluate any significant trends, variances, or changes.

7. Review the information for extensions of credit to officers and directors of other banks and investigate for any circumstances that may indicate preferential treatment.

8. Review information provided for DRC-related suspense accounts and discuss with management any large or stale items in the accounts. Perform additional procedures, as deemed appropriate.

9. Determine compliance with laws and regulations pertaining to specific DRC products and services, as described below.

   - For 12 CFR 215, 12 USC 375a, "Loans to Executive Officers of Bank," and 12 USC 375b, "Extensions of Credit to Executive Officers, Directors, and Principal Shareholders of Member Banks." Per 12 USC 1468(b), the aforementioned sections of 12 USC 375a and 12 USC 375b apply to all savings associations "in the same manner and to the same extent" as if the savings association were a member bank. Per 12 CFR 163.43, savings associations are subject to Regulation O.

     Provide the examiner assigned to "Loan Portfolio Management" outstanding balances on DRC products and services for advances to executive officers, directors, and principal shareholders and their related interests to ensure they are included in the review for compliance with Regulation O.

Otherwise, review information received from the examiner assigned "Loan Portfolio Management," including participations and loans sold, and

- test the accuracy and completeness of the loans to executive officers, directors, and principal shareholders and their related interests by looking to see if the information includes DRC products and services for the individuals and credits sampled.
- review credit files to determine whether required information is available.

- For 12 USC 84 "Lending limits" (national banks), 12 USC 1464(u) "Limits on loans to one borrower" (federal savings associations), and 12 CFR 32 "Lending limits," determine compliance with the lending limits for aggregate loans to customers. These laws and regulations apply to extensions of credit to all customers of the bank. 12 USC 84 is made applicable to federal savings associations by 12 USC 1464(u).

- For 12 USC 1464(c)(2)(A) and 12 CFR 160.30, endnote 19 (federal savings associations), determine compliance with the statutory investment limit in commercial loans. Overdraft credit extended by a federal savings association relating to commercial demand deposit accounts is considered a commercial loan for purposes of determining the association's percentage of assets limitation.

- For 31 CFR 1010.410(a), "Records to be Made and Retained by Financial Institutions," review operating procedures and credit file documentation and determine whether the bank retains a record of each extension of credit of more than $10,000 that specify the name and address of the customer, the amount of the credit, the nature and purpose of the credit, and the date of the credit.

10. Assess the quality, accuracy, and completeness of MIS reports and other analyses used to manage the DRC collections process.

11. Determine what system(s) the bank uses to recover DRC charged-off accounts and balances and whether they interface with the bank's collection management system(s). If not, determine how the recovery unit gathers and uses information about prior collection activities.

12. Determine whether customer service or any department other than collections can initiate DRC collection activities. If so, determine whether appropriate monitoring MIS are in place to monitor volumes and credit performance of accounts in collection activities initiated outside of collections.

Profitability

Objective: To assess management's ability to accurately calculate the profitability of DRC products and services while also assessing the quantity, quality, and sustainability of earnings from DRC products and services.

1. Review profitability statements for DRC activities to evaluate major costs and fee income items in relation to overall profitability. Determine the impact of DRC losses and fraud losses on line-of-business profitability. Consider the level and trend of charge-offs and recoveries on DRC operating performance.

2. Review operating results for DRC activities for the most recent year-end and the current year to date. Determine whether there is a profit or loss and the extent to which the bank is relying on fee income generated from DRC products and services. Assess whether the bank has an over-reliance on fee income from any single DRC product. Evaluate whether the bank considers the significance of a particular product and monitors for potentially undue reliance on fees generated by that product for its revenue and earnings.

3. If the DRC operation is unprofitable, determine the bank's appetite, plan, and rationale for continuing to offer unprofitable products and services, or assess the bank's plans for bringing certain products and services, and the operation to a profitable status.

4. Review the budgeting process for the DRC area and investigate any significant variances between budget and actual performance. Determine whether the department is expected to meet this year's budget and, if not, why not.

5. Evaluate the MIS used in determining the department's profitability.

6. Determine how management determines costs—that is, whether it uses actual or estimated costs—and whether the methodology is appropriate.

7. Review the bank's pricing policies and evaluate the bank's pricing methods. If the bank offers reduced rates based on other existing banking relationships, evaluate the risks and rewards.

8. Determine which personnel have the authority to set pricing variables and how management monitors the pricing process.

9. If the bank relies on third parties in connection with DRC products and services, coordinate with the examiner reviewing third-party relationships and determine whether pricing programs are used and whether pricing is tied to other services.

Risk Management and Control Systems

Objective: To assess the adequacy of the bank's processes for identifying, measuring, monitoring, and controlling risk related to DRC activity by reviewing the effectiveness of risk management and other control functions.

1. Consider whether processes are effective, adequately communicated to appropriate staff, and consistent with underlying bank policies. Review any written procedures and processes for DRC. Discuss processes with management and department heads to determine how policy requirements and changes are communicated.

2. Determine whether internal controls are in place and functioning as designed. Complete the internal control questionnaire (ICQ) for CC, if necessary. Review any special reports the bank may use for internal control purposes, and hold discussions with management, as appropriate.

3. Assess and review the scope, frequency, effectiveness, and independence of the internal and external audit of the DRC area.

   - Review audit reports, work papers, and management's responses to any issues. Determine the status of corrective actions as appropriate.
   - Determine whether internal auditors review major services provided by third-party organizations for DRC, if applicable.
   - Determine whether audits address appropriate operational areas for DRC.
   - Assess the internal or external auditor's knowledge of the DRC area and whether the auditor's knowledge is adequate to perform an effective review.
   - Determine whether audit findings and the status of responses to audit findings are relayed to the board.

4. Determine how the bank establishes parameters for exceptions to DRC policies and procedures and the approval process for exceptions, if applicable.

5. Evaluate monitoring systems' effectiveness in identifying, measuring, and tracking exceptions to policies and established limits.

6. Assess the adequacy of the overall MIS information by doing the following:

   - Review the MIS reports management routinely uses and determine whether the reports adequately inform management of the risk posed by DRC products and services.
   - Determine whether adequate processes exist to ensure data integrity and report accuracy.
   - Determine whether key management reports are clearly labeled, dated, maintained, and updated.
   - Determine whether reports are produced to track volume and performance by product, channel, or marketing initiative.

- Determine whether reports are available to track performance trends, delinquency, and quality.
- Review reports to the board and determine whether the information the directors receive is timely, accurate, and useful. At a minimum, reports should include information for each portfolio product, number of accounts and total balances, delinquency and charge-off information, fraud activity, and risk levels and trends for the DRC area.
- Evaluate systems planning to determine whether MIS and reporting needs are adequately researched and developed before new products and services are rolled out. Specifically, determine whether the systems and reports are adequate to supervise and administer new products and services.
- Review the adequacy of MIS reports pertaining to fraud. Determine whether the information is sufficient to monitor fraud and the effectiveness of fraud controls, including the appropriate filing of suspicious activity reports (SAR).

7. Determine whether the bank has appropriate DRC tracking and reporting systems (e.g., by product type) and whether management regularly monitors and analyzes that information, including

- utilization rate of the CC and DAP as a percentage of the approved credit limit, and for ODP, as a percentage of deposit accounts.
- timeliness of repayments.
- charges or fees per account and as a percentage of average account balance.
- losses as a percentage of the specific product by number of accounts and in dollars.

8. Review the bank's call report to ensure that the bank is treating assets and any losses associated with DRC appropriately. Specifically, confirm that

- DRC assets are treated as "other consumer loans" on Schedule RC-C.
- if the bank advises the customer of the available amount of ODP, the unadvanced portions (with legally binding commitments) are reported as unused commitments on Schedule RC-L.
- principal losses and recoveries related to these accounts go through the allowance for loan and lease losses (ALLL) and are shown on Schedule RI-B.
- losses associated with fees are reversed against the income account in which originally recognized (if in the same accounting period) or are charged against a loss allowance for uncollectible fees.

9. Determine whether the scope and frequency of fraud reviews are adequate. Assess the bank's processes if potential fraud is uncovered.

Perform verification procedures if the reports and trial balances contain unusual information or information that cannot be readily explained.

Third-Party Management

Objective: To determine the extent of all third-party relationships[19] in DRC and evaluate the effectiveness of management's oversight and risk management processes.

1. Determine what third-party relationships the bank uses for DRC. Identify the role the third parties play and the activities or services performed.

2. Assess the rationale behind management's decision to use third-party providers for DRC and determine whether the bank conducted an appropriate due diligence review.

3. Evaluate whether the bank periodically reviews its third-party servicers and, if so, the frequency and content of the reviews. Information available for the review of third-party servicers may include audit reports, financial statements, third-party operational reviews, disaster contingency plans, and reports of bank regulatory agencies.

4. Review major contracts of third-party relationships to assess the following information:

   - Terms specifying financial compensation, payment arrangements, and price changes.
   - Reasonableness of the compensation agreement. If there are income-sharing provisions, determine whether the provisions are equitable to the bank and whether the third-party relationship shares not only income but also costs (e.g., participates in credit losses, receives less income).
   - Provisions prohibiting the third party from assigning the agreement to any other party.
   - Frequency and means of communications and monitoring activities of each party.
   - Specific work the third party performs.
   - Whether the contract addresses compliance with the specific laws and regulations and is consistent with supervisory guidance and self-regulatory standards applicable to the activities involved.
   - Whether the contract states the bank has the right to monitor on an ongoing basis the third party's compliance with applicable laws, regulations, and policies and requires remediation if issues arise.
   - Whether the contract provides for the confidential treatment of records.
   - Record-keeping requirements for each party and whether the parties have access to each other's records.
   - Whether the bank or the third party is responsible for responding to customer complaints. If the third party is responsible for customer complaints, whether the contract includes provisions that ensure the third party receives and responds timely to customer complaints and forwards a copy of each complaint and response to the bank.
   - Whether the contract stipulates when and how the third party should notify the bank of its intent to use a subcontractor, whether the contract specifies the activities that

---

[19] OCC Bulletin 2013-29, "Third-Party Relationships: Risk Management Guidance."

cannot be subcontracted or whether the bank prohibits the third party from subcontracting activities to certain locations or specific subcontractors.

- Responsibility for audits and whether the bank has the right to audit the third party.
- Notification requirements for system changes that could affect procedures and reports.
- Whether the contract includes requirements for the regular and timely submission of the third party's financial information and, if the third party is involved with the ongoing administration or servicing of the product, whether the contract allows the bank to audit the third party at will.
- Whether the contract includes a reasonable right to cancel and whether termination clauses are one-sided in the third party's favor.
- Whether contractual penalties for terminating the contract seem reasonable.
- Whether the contracts contain the appropriate signatures.

5. List third-party relationships that have provided contingency plan information. Review the bank's analysis of contingency plans to determine adequacy. If an analysis does not exist, review the reasonableness of contingency plans.

6. Determine whether third-party contingency plans are adequately considered in the bank's overall contingency plan.

7. Determine whether the management of DRC products and services requires the third party to adopt a written action plan when results fall below the bank's standards, are inconsistent with supervisory guidance, or violate legal standards.

8. Determine whether the bank keeps contracts on file for each third-party relationship used for the DRC program, the location of original contracts for third-party providers, and whether the bank requires that the contracts be maintained in a secure, fire-protected area.

9. Obtain a report that shows the volume of activity with each third-party relationship. Review third-party relationships that have a significant volume of activity (transactions or dollar amount).

10. Review a sample of third-party relationship files. Evaluate whether the information in the files is appropriate in light of the significance of the third party's activities and risk posed to the bank and check for compliance with the bank's policy.

Conclusions

Conclusion: The aggregate level of each associated risk is (low, moderate, or high). The direction of each associated risk is (increasing, stable, or decreasing).

Objective: To determine, document, and communicate overall findings and conclusions regarding the examination of DRC.

1. Determine preliminary examination findings and conclusions and discuss with the EIC, including

   - quantity of associated risks (as noted in the "Introduction" section).
   - quality of risk management.
   - aggregate level and direction of associated risks.
   - overall risk in DRC.
   - violations and other concerns.

Summary of Risks Associated With DRC				
Risk category	Quantity of risk (Low, moderate, high)	Quality of risk management (Weak, satisfactory, strong)	Aggregate level of risk (Low, moderate, high)	Direction of risk (Increasing, stable, decreasing)
Credit				
Liquidity				
Operational				
Compliance				
Strategic				
Reputation				

2. If substantive safety and soundness concerns remain unresolved that may have a material adverse effect on the bank, further expand the scope of the examination by completing verification procedures.

3. Share substantive consumer protection concerns that are identified or remain unresolved with the EIC or lead compliance examiner for direction and appropriate course of action.

4. Discuss examination findings with bank management, including violations, recommendations, and conclusions about risks and risk management practices. If necessary, obtain commitments for corrective action.

5. Compose conclusion comments, highlighting any issues that should be included in the report of examination (ROE). If necessary, compose a matters requiring attention comment.

6. Update the OCC's information system and any applicable ROE schedules or tables.

7. Write a memorandum specifically setting out what the OCC should do to effectively supervise DRC in the bank, including time periods, staffing, and workdays required.

8. Update, organize, and reference work papers in accordance with OCC policy.

9. Ensure that any paper or electronic media that contain sensitive bank or customer information are appropriately disposed of or secured.

Internal Control Questionnaire for Check Credit

An ICQ helps an examiner assess a bank's internal controls for an area. ICQs typically address standard controls that provide day-to-day protection of bank assets and financial records. The examiner decides the extent to which it is necessary to complete or update ICQs during examination planning or after reviewing the findings and conclusions of the core assessment.

Although this ICQ is specifically designed for CC, to the extent that the following questions are applicable, examiners may also apply them to DAP and ODP.

CC Policies

1. Has the board of directors, consistent with its duties and responsibilities, adopted written CC policies that establish

    - procedures for reviewing CC applications or eligibility where applications are not required?
    - standards for determining credit lines and limits?
    - minimum standards for documentation?

2. Are CC policies reviewed at least annually to determine whether they are compatible with changing market conditions and legal requirements?

CC Records

3. Is the preparation and posting of subsidiary CC records performed or reviewed by persons who do not also

    - issue official checks or drafts singly?
    - handle cash?

4. Are the subsidiary CC records reconciled daily to the appropriate general ledger accounts and are reconciling items investigated by persons who do not also handle cash?

5. Are delinquent account collection requests and past-due notices checked to the trial balances used in reconciling CC subsidiary records to general ledger accounts and are they handled only by persons who do not also handle cash?

6. Are inquiries about credit balances received and investigated by persons who do not also handle cash?

7. Are documents supporting recorded CC adjustments checked or tested subsequently by persons who do not also handle cash? (If not, briefly explain.)

8. Is a daily record maintained summarizing transaction details—e.g., credits extended, payments received, and interest or fees collected—to support applicable general ledger account entries?

9. Are frequent note and liability ledger trial balances prepared and reconciled with controlling accounts by employees who do not process or record credit transactions?

10. Are suspense accounts reviewed daily for timely disposition of all items?

11. Are authorized signatures required to effect a status change regarding individual customer accounts?

12. Is an exception report produced that encompasses extensions, renewals, and any factors that would result in a change in customer account status and is it reviewed by operating management?

13. Is an overdue-accounts report generated frequently? If so, how often?

Interest and Service Fees

14. Is the preparation and posting of interest or service fee records performed or reviewed by persons who do not also

    • issue official checks or drafts singly?
    • handle cash?

15. Are any independent interest and service fee computations made and compared or tested to initial interest and service fee records by persons who do not also

    • issue official checks or drafts singly?
    • handle cash?

Other

16. Are statements of balances and payments due issued at least monthly?

17. If the CC is established in conjunction with a demand account, are combined demand deposit and credit statements issued?

18. If the CC (regarding available checks to the customer) is separate from the customer's demand account, but is paid through the demand account, are notices of transfer from the CC cash reserve to the demand account delivered on a timely basis to the customer?

19. Are all internally prepared entries affecting customer account records approved by an officer?

20. Are customers prohibited from exceeding their maximum approved lines?

- If not, is the allowed overline amount a percentage of their maximum approved credit line? If so, what is the stated percentage?

21. Are the following reports prepared for internal use in the department and monitored:

- Overlimit and overline balances?
- Stagnant maximum usage balances?
- Inactive suspect accounts (accounts for which payments are made by drawing on reserve)?

22. Are the above reports reviewed for accuracy periodically by someone independent of the CC function?

23. Are customers forbidden to make payments by drawing against a CC reserve?

- If not, how many payments may be made by drawing against the CC reserve before a warning is issued to the customer?

24. Do operating procedures require that simultaneous drawing and payment postings to the same account be reported to department management?

25. Is a completed application obtained from each customer that includes the following (specific information for the application and the application process may vary by product and underwriting or credit eligibility criteria):

- Name?
- Address?
- Number of dependents?
- Occupation?
- Length of employment?
- Income?

26. Are credit limits varied according to the customer's repayment ability?

- If so, does the bank conduct an analysis of the customer's financial capacity, including income levels?

27. Are credit limit approvals made by an officer or employee granted credit authority by the board of directors?

28. Are credit investigations performed on every applicant before a CC is approved?

29. Are credit reports and investigations updated periodically? If so, what is or what are the periodic basis or criteria used to determine when updated credit reports and investigations should occur?

30. Is each credit line evidenced by a properly completed credit agreement?

31. Are credit lines periodically reviewed for appropriateness of the amount of the line?

32. Is additional credit review undertaken if the customer requests a credit line increase?

33. Are procedures in effect to review credit lines if the bank becomes aware of a change in the financial status or creditworthiness of a borrower?

34. Do controls exist to prohibit the opening of more than one specific type of CC account for any one customer?

35. Are exception reports reviewed and initialed by an officer daily?

36. Is a regular review made of all past-due accounts?

37. Is a customer contact record maintained for each collection account with appropriately detailed comments and date of contact?

38. Are collectors required to issue pre-numbered receipts when payments are received?

39. Is customer contact rotated between collectors?

40. Are procedures in effect for establishing employee accounts?

41. Are employee accounts periodically reviewed?

42. If employees are permitted to maintain CC accounts, are procedures in effect to determine whether accounts are being used to conceal shortages during audits of those employees?

Conclusion

43. Is the foregoing information an adequate basis for evaluating internal controls, in that there are no significant additional internal auditing procedures, accounting controls, administrative controls, or other circumstances that impair any controls or mitigate any weaknesses indicated above? (Explain negative answers briefly and indicate conclusions regarding the effects on specific examination or verification procedures.)

44. Based on the answers to the foregoing questions, internal control for CC is considered _____ (strong, satisfactory, or weak).

Verification Procedures

Verification procedures are used to verify the existence of assets and liabilities or test the reliability of financial records. Examiners generally do not perform verification procedures as part of a typical examination. Rather, verification procedures are performed when substantive safety and soundness concerns are identified that are not mitigated by the bank's risk management systems and internal controls.

1. Test the addition of the trial balance and the reconciliation of the trial balance to the general ledger.

2. Using appropriate sampling techniques, select accounts from the trial balance including customer outstanding balance and approved limit for the customer, and

   - prepare and mail confirmation forms to ask customers to confirm balances and credit limits as of the last statement date.
   - after a reasonable time, mail second requests for any confirmations not returned by the customers.
   - follow up on any no-replies or exceptions received and resolve differences.

3. If the bank charges a fee for DRC services,

   - using the selected accounts, check computation of the latest charges.
   - trace charges to posting in appropriate general ledger income account.
   - review monthly income amounts posted to the general ledger for reasonableness relative to the number of DRC accounts handled.

4. Obtain or prepare a schedule showing the amount of monthly interest and fee income and the DRC credit balances at the end of each month since the preceding examination and investigate significant fluctuations or trends.

Appendixes

Appendix A: Sample Request Letter

Deposit-Related Credit Request Letter

Please provide copies of the following:

Management and Board Supervision

1. Current organizational chart for the DRC department or those overseeing DRC activity (hereinafter, DRC department).

2. Résumés of all principals in the DRC department.

3. Job descriptions of all principal positions in the DRC department.

4. DRC department's strategic and business plans and budgets.

5. Management's annual analysis of capital adequacy or capital allocation relative to the risk profile of DRC activities.

6. Two most recent sets of recurring management reports related to DRC activity reviewed by management and/or the board of directors.

7. Report on new DRC activity or management summaries of DRC activity for the previous three months.

8. Any credit risk management reports for DRC.

9. Concentration reports for DRC by state or geographic area or industry.

Underwriting and Eligibility

10. A listing of all insider-related DRC customers.

11. Samples of customer agreements, including deposit account agreements eligible for ODP, and applications related to DRC.

12. List of all DRC reserves.

Profitability

13. Profitability report for the DRC department for the most recent year-end and the current year to date.

14. Current fee schedule and definitions of fees charged for DRC.

15. Profitability reports by DRC product segment.

Third-Party Relationships

16. List of third parties used for DRC activity by name and address and a description of services provided. Are any third-party arrangements new to the bank within the last 12 months? If so, please provide an electronic copy of the contract with the third party.

17. List of any credit relationships with third parties associated with DRC activities, including credit terms and amounts.

Risk Management

18. Management summary of underwriting exceptions/overrides for DRC activity.

19. Brief description of the fraud-monitoring process, the systems and reports used, prioritization of investigations, and staffing involved in the process for DRC activity.

20. Representative sample of daily fraud-monitoring reports for DRC activity.

21. Fraud loss history for DRC for the most recent year-end and year to date. Were suspicious activity reports filed for the fraud losses identified?

22. Credit loss history for DRC for the most recent year-end and year to date.

23. Any additional risk analysis or reports used to evaluate DRC activity apart from daily monitoring reports.

Audit

24. Most recent internal or external audit reports related to DRC activity and management's response.

Loan Review

25. Copies of internal loan review and ODP reports for the DRC activity. Also, provide any management responses for these reports.

Please Make the Following Available Upon Our Arrival at the Bank:

26. DRC policy and procedure manuals.

27. Committee minutes for DRC activities.

28. All third-party credit files, including current financial statements for parties providing services to DRC activities.

29. All third-party written contracts and agreements related to DRC products and services and agreements between third parties and the bank's data processor(s).

30. Disaster contingency plans for third-party organizations that provide DRC-related services and bank management's review of the plans.

31. Internal or external auditor work papers from review of DRC activity.

Appendix B: Checklist for Deposit Advance Products

	Yes	No	Examiner comments
Does the bank monitor for repeated or extended use of DAP credit?			
Are eligibility and underwriting criteria designed to assure that the extension of credit, including all associated fees and expenses, can be repaid according to its terms while allowing the customer to continue to meet typical recurring and other necessary expenses, as well as other outstanding debt obligations?			
Does the bank maintain appropriate criteria to prevent churning and prolonged use of DAP credits?			
Does underwriting for DAP credits occur prior to opening such accounts and does monitoring occur on an ongoing basis?			
Are bank policies regarding the underwriting of DAPs written and approved by the bank's board of directors and consistent with the bank's general underwriting standards and risk appetite?			
Do written underwriting policies for DAPs include:			
• The length of a customer's deposit relationship with the bank (no less than six months)?			
• Ineligibility for DAPs for customers with delinquent or adversely classified credits with the bank that is offering the DAP?			
• An analysis of the customer's financial capacity including income levels?			
• An analysis of the customer's account for recurring deposits (inflows) and checks/credit/customer withdrawals (outflows) over at least six consecutive months?			
• The exclusion of items from lines of credit, including overdrafts, and drafts from savings, from inflows (these items should not be counted as inflows)?			
• Consideration of the customer's net surplus or deficit at the end of each of the preceding six months without reliance on a six-month transaction average?			
• A cooling off period of at least one monthly statement cycle after the repayment of a DAP should be completed before another advance may be extended in order to avoid repeated use of the short-term product?			
• A full underwriting reassessment in compliance with the bank's underwriting policies before determining whether the amount of credit available to a customer can or cannot be increased?			
• That any increase in the credit limit should not be automatic and should be initiated by a request from the customer?			
• As part of the underwriting for this product, that the bank should, no less than every six months, reevaluate the customer's eligibility and capacity for this product?			

	Yes	No	Examiner comments
• That a bank should identify the risks that could negatively affect a customer's eligibility to receive additional DAPs (such as repeated overdrafts or evidence that a customer is overextended with respect to total credit obligations)?			
Higher capital requirements generally apply to credit portfolios that exhibit higher-risk characteristics and are subject to less stringent credit underwriting characteristics. How does the bank arrive at the capital level held for the DAP portfolio?			
Fees associated with DAPs should be based on safe and sound banking principles. What fees or fee structure does the bank utilize for DAPs and does it appear reasonable?			
Does the bank monitor for any undue reliance on fees generated by DAPs for its revenue and earnings? If it does monitor for undue reliance on fees, how does it monitor and how frequently does it monitor for undue reliance on fees?			
Is the ALLL adequate for estimated credit losses for the DAP portfolio?			
Does the bank have methodologies and analyses in place to demonstrate and document that the level of the ALLL is appropriate?			
Has the bank implemented effective compliance management systems, processes, and procedures to mitigate risks appropriately?			
Is the bank in compliance with applicable consumer protection statutes and regulations, including TILA, EFTA, TISA, ECOA, and Section 5 of the FTC Act?			
In the review of a bank's relationships with third parties involved in the bank's DAP, is the bank assuming more risk than it can identify, monitor, and manage?			
Has bank management allocated sufficient and qualified staff to monitor risks posed by third-party relationships, excessive usage by customers, and excessive risk taking by the bank?			
Have examiners identified high-risk situations associated with third-party relationships that necessitate examiners conducting on-site third-party reviews under specific authorities granted to the OCC?			
Has bank management established controls and implemented a rigorous analytical process to identify, measure, monitor, and manage the risks associated with DAPs?			
Does the bank maintain adequate oversight of DAPs and adequate quality control over products and services to minimize exposure to potential significant financial loss, reputation damage, and supervisory action?			
Does the bank's compliance management system ensure continuing compliance with applicable federal and state laws, and regulations, as well as internal policies and procedures?			
Has management provided the appropriate oversight and allocated sufficient and qualified staff to monitor deposit advance programs?			

	Yes	No	Examiner comments
Are results of oversight activities, including identified weaknesses that should be documented and promptly addressed, reported periodically to the bank's board of directors or designated committee?			

Appendix C: Abbreviations

ACH	automated clearing house
ALLL	allowance for loan and lease losses
APR	annual percentage rate
ATM	automated teller machine
Board	Board of Governors of the Federal Reserve System
call report	Consolidated Reports of Condition and Income
CAMELS	capital adequacy, asset quality, management, earnings, liquidity, and sensitivity to market risk
CC	check credit
CFPB	Consumer Financial Protection Bureau
CFR	Code of Federal Regulations
DAP	deposit advance product
Dodd–Frank	Dodd-Frank Wall Street Reform and Consumer Protection Act of 2010
DRC	deposit-related credit
ECOA	Equal Credit Opportunity Act of 1974
EFTA	Electronic Fund Transfer Act of 1978
EIC	examiner-in-charge
FDIC	Federal Deposit Insurance Corporation
FFIEC	Federal Financial Institutions Examination Council
FTC	Federal Trade Commission
GAAP	generally accepted accounting principles
ICQ	internal control questionnaire
ISAE	International Standard on Assurance Engagements
IT	information technology
MIS	management information systems
OCC	Office of the Comptroller of the Currency
ODP	overdraft protection
OTS	Office of Thrift Supervision
ROE	report of examination
SAR	suspicious activity report
SSAE	Statement on Standards for Attestation Engagement
TILA	Truth in Lending Act of 1968
TISA	Truth in Savings Act of 1991
UDAP	unfair or deceptive acts or practices
USC	U.S. Code

References

Laws

12 USC 24, "Corporate Powers of Associations" (national banks)

12 USC 84, "Lending Limits" (national banks) (made applicable to federal savings associations by 12 USC 1464(u))

12 USC 161, "Reports to the Comptroller of the Currency" (national banks)

12 USC 375a, "Loans to Executive Officers of Bank" (national banks) (made applicable to federal savings associations by 12 USC 1468(b))

12 USC 375b, "Extensions of Credit to Executive Officers, Directors, and Principal Shareholders of Member Banks" (national banks) (made applicable to federal savings associations by 12 USC 1468(b))

12 USC 1464(c), "Loans and Investments" (federal savings associations)

12 USC 1464(d)(7), "Regulation and Examination of Savings Association Service Companies, Subsidiaries, and Service Providers" (federal savings associations)

12 USC 1464(u), "Limits on Loans to One Borrower" (federal savings associations)

12 USC 1464(v), "Reports of Condition" (federal savings associations)

12 USC 1468(b), "Extensions of Credit to Executive Officers, Directors, and Principal Shareholders" (federal savings associations)

12 USC 1867(c), "Services Performed by Contract or Otherwise" (national banks and federal savings associations)

12 USC 4301, "Truth in Savings" (national banks and federal savings associations)

12 USC 5514(e); 5515(d); 5516(e), "Service Providers" (national banks and federal savings associations)

15 USC 45, "Unfair Methods of Competition Unlawful; Prevention by Commission" (UDAP) (national banks and federal savings associations)

15 USC 1601, "Truth in Lending Act" (national banks and federal savings associations)

15 USC 1691, "Equal Credit Opportunity Act" (national banks and federal savings associations)

15 USC 1693, "Electronic Fund Transfer Act" (national banks and federal savings associations)

31 USC 5315, "Reports on Foreign Currency Transactions" (national banks and federal savings associations)

Regulations

12 CFR 3, "Capital Adequacy Standards" (national banks and federal savings associations)

12 CFR 7.4002, "National Bank Charges" (national banks)

12 CFR 21.11, "Suspicious Activity Report" (national banks)

12 CFR 32, "Lending Limits" (national banks and federal savings associations)

12 CFR 160.30, "General Lending and Investment Powers of Federal Savings Associations" (federal savings associations)

12 CFR 163.43, "Loans by Savings Associations to Their Executive Officers, Directors and Principal Shareholders" (federal savings associations)

12 CFR 163.180, "Suspicious Activity Report" (federal savings associations)

12 CFR 167, "Capital" (federal savings associations)

12 CFR 215, "Loans to Executive Officers, Directors, and Principal Shareholders of Member Banks (Regulation O)" (national banks and federal savings associations)

12 CFR 1002, "Equal Credit Opportunity Act, Regulation B" (national banks and federal savings associations)

12 CFR 1005, "Electronic Fund Transfers, Regulation E" (national banks and federal savings associations)

12 CFR 1026, "Truth in Lending, Regulation Z" (national banks and federal savings associations)

12 CFR 1030, "Truth in Savings, Regulation DD" (national banks and federal savings associations)

31 CFR 1010.410(a), "Records to be Made and Retained by Financial Institutions" (national banks and federal savings associations)

Comptroller's Handbook

Examination Process
"Bank Supervision Process"
"Community Bank Supervision"
"Large Bank Supervision"

Consumer Compliance
"Community Reinvestment Act Examination Procedures"
"Compliance Management System"
"Depository Services"
"Fair Credit Reporting"
"Fair Lending"
"Servicemembers Civil Relief Act of 2003"
"Truth in Lending Act"

Safety and Soundness, Asset Quality
"Allowance for Loan and Lease Losses"
"Commercial Loans"

OCC Issuances

Advisory Letter 2000-7, "Abusive Lending Practices" (July 25, 2000) (national banks and federal savings associations)

Advisory Letter 2002-3, "Guidance on Unfair or Deceptive Acts or Practices" (March 22, 2002) (national banks and federal savings associations)

OCC Bulletin 1998-3, "Technology Risk Management: Guidance for Bankers and Examiners" (February 4, 1998) (national banks and federal savings associations)

OCC Bulletin 2000-20, "Uniform Retail Credit Classification and Account Management Policy: Policy Implementation" (June 20, 2000) (national banks and federal savings associations)

OCC Bulletin 2001-6, "Subprime Lending: Expanded Guidance for Subprime Lending Programs" (January 31, 2001) (national banks and federal savings associations)

OCC Bulletin 2001-37, "Policy Statement on Allowance for Loan and Lease Losses Methodologies and Documentation for Banks and Savings Institutions: ALLL Methodologies and Documentation" (July 20, 2001) (national banks and federal savings associations)

OCC Bulletin 2005-9, "Overdraft Protection Programs: Interagency Guidance" (April 6, 2005) (national banks and federal savings associations)

OCC Bulletin 2010-15, "Overdraft Protection: Opt-In Requirements and Related Marketing Issues" (April 12, 2010) (national banks)

OCC Bulletin 2010-24, "Incentive Compensation: Interagency Guidance on Sound Incentive Compensation Policies" (June 30, 2010) (national banks and federal savings associations)

OCC Bulletin 2012-34, "Supervision of Technology Service Providers: FFIEC IT Examination Handbook Booklet Revision and Administrative Guidelines for Interagency Supervisory Programs" (October 31, 2012) (national banks and federal savings associations)

OCC Bulletin 2013-23, "Regulatory Capital Rule: Final Rulemaking" (October 11, 2013) (national banks and federal savings associations)

OCC Bulletin 2013-29, "Third-Party Relationships: Risk Management Guidance" (October 30, 2013) (national banks and federal savings associations)

OCC Bulletin 2013-40, "Deposit Advance Products: Final Supervisory Guidance" (December 26, 2013) (national banks and federal savings associations)

OTS Examination Handbook section 1354, "Unfair or Deceptive Acts or Practices, Federal Trade Commission Act, Section 5" (May 2010) and related "Program" (March 2011) and "Questionnaire" (May 2010) (federal savings associations)

FFIEC

"Administrative Guidelines—Implementation of Interagency Programs for the Supervision of Technology Service Providers" (October 2012)

Federal Regulatory Agencies' Administrative Guidelines—Implementation of Interagency Programs for the Supervision of Technology Service Providers (issued jointly by the OCC, FDIC, and Board) (October 2012) (national banks and federal savings associations)

FFIEC Information Technology Examination Handbook

"Outsourcing Technology Services" (June 2004)
"Retail Payment Systems" (February 2010)
"Supervision of Technology Service Providers" (October 2012)

Other

American Institute of Certified Public Accountants, Accounting Standards Board, "Statement on Standards for Attestation Engagement No. 16, Reporting on Controls at a Service Organization" (SSAE 16)

International Auditing and Assurance Standards Board, "International Standard on Assurance Engagements" (ISAE 3402)